Humankind-ness

when you share your goodness with
others your life is a quote

a compilation of timeless wisdom

Natasha Amastar

Cover chalkboard photo by Indran Naick
Rajanata Publishing Company

Print books and ebooks are available online at:
Amazon, Kindle, iTunes, iBookstore, Barnes and Noble and others

Inquires and correspondence should be addressed to:

Natasha Amastar
Email: toncebaby@hotmail.com
Phone Number: (310) 556-2295

Printed in the United States of America

Book created in 2008
First edition, January 2014

10 9 8 7 6 5 4 3 2 1

ISBN-13: 9798986608686

Table of Contents

About the Author
My Message

I have been fighting for my life for the last six years. Due to a number of challenges, I have been unable to achieve the goals I initially set out for myself. From an early age I have wanted to earn a Ph.D. in Psychology and to teach at a college or university. I have wanted to teach about the pain that is caused by child abuse and neglect and how that pain can contribute to a waste of our human potential. Mostly, I have wanted to teach about how to raise children in loving, non-violent homes where they have a voice, and where they are able to grow up to be feeling people who are kind and compassionate.

I may never stand in front of students in a classroom, but I believe I have found another way to teach. This book embodies the messages that I wish to share with the world. The messages awaken, enlighten, and empower us to reach our maximum potential so we do not have to waste one minute of our time here on Earth.

It is my hope that you take these messages and live them, because, when you share your goodness with others your life is a quote!

Preface

Quotes are like bolts of lightning that strike us with profound emotion as we reflect upon the human condition. Quotes electrify the mind, energize the heart and illuminate the soul. The quotes in this book span a period of six thousand years and capture the revelations of mankind. Let each one be the spark that further ignites your flame.

The book opens with quotes about Purpose that highlight the importance of living life with significance. Then, quotes on Humanology and Challenge consider the various aspects of human nature that often make it difficult to fulfill Purpose. These are followed by messages of Inspiration and Guidance that encourage and uplift, paving the way for passages about Service and Gratitude. Finally, words of Wisdom and Consciousness open the door to quotes on Justice and Human Rights that are also depicted in the Graffiti Walls.

There is only one kind... Humankind-ness

I dedicate this book to all of humanity; past, present and future

May these QUOTES lead us on a QUEST

Purpose

The world is my classroom, everyone is my classmate and the learning never ends!
~Natasha Amastar (1)

You must learn to live and live to learn. ~Tanner Leiderman (2)

Live on purpose. Live with purpose. Live your purpose. ~Ralph Marston (3)

Each minute of life should be a divine quest. ~Paramahansa Yogananda (4)

God's work must truly be our own. ~John F. Kennedy (5)

What can't be done must be done. ~Natasha Amastar(6)

Change will not come if we wait for some other person or some other time. We are the ones we've been waiting for. We are the change that we seek. ~Barack Obama (7)

The purpose of life is to have a life of purpose. ~Natasha Amastar (8)

And in the end, it's not the years in your life that count, it's the life in your years.
~Abraham Lincoln (9)

Your greatest self has been waiting your whole life; don't make it wait any longer.
~Steve Maraboli (10)

To live is the rarest thing in the world. Most people exist, that is all. ~Oscar Wilde (11)

The tragedy of life is what dies inside a man while he lives. ~Albert Einstein (12)

Every man is guilty of all the things he did not do. ~Voltaire (13)

The most destructive force in the universe is regret. ~Unknown (14)

Your inner purpose is to awaken. It is as simple as that. ~Eckhart Tolle (15)

Don't just think about it, be about it. ~Tanner Leiderman (16)

You are what you do, not what you say you'll do. ~Carl Jung (17)

I hope that I may always desire more than I can accomplish. ~Maya Angelou (18)

Dream so big that it takes three lifetimes to fulfill. ~Natasha Amastar (19)

Our prime purpose in this life is to help others. And if you can't help them, at least don't hurt them. ~Dalai Lama (20)

Purpose is the place where your deep gladness meets the world's needs. ~Frederick Buechner (21)

My legacy is to help you leave your legacy. ~Blythe Daniel(22)

No one really knows why they are alive until they know what they would die for. ~Martin Luther King, Jr. (23)

Great minds have purposes; others have wishes. ~Washington Irving (24)

Your goals, minus your doubts, equal your reality. ~Ralph Marston (25)

If we did the things we are capable of, we would astound ourselves. ~Thomas Edison (26)

Well done is better than well said. ~Benjamin Franklin(27)

My actions are my only true belongings. ~Thich Nhat Hanh (28)

The search for the meaning of life gives life its meaning. ~David Daniel (29)

If I can stop one heart from breaking, I shall not live in vain. If I can ease one life the aching, or cool one pain, or help one fainting robin unto his nest again, I shall not live in vain. ~Emily Dickinson (30)

A life is not important except in the impact it has on other lives. ~Jackie Robinson (31)

Working hard doesn't make you successful. Working right does. ~Asher Monroe Book (32)

Life is tragic for those who have plenty to live on and nothing to live for. ~Unknown (33)

The best way to predict the future is to invent it. ~Alan Kay (34)

My goals are like mile markers on an endless highway. ~Tanner Leiderman (35)

At the end of the day Twitter has it wrong. We should all be leaders, not followers. ~Hector David Jr. (36)

I may not be the chosen one, but I have chosen to be the one. ~Unknown (37)

Be married to your purpose and you will have a blissful life. ~Blythe Daniel (38)

My life is my message. ~Mahatma Gandhi (39)

Your sole purpose is to find your soul purpose. ~Natasha Amastar (40)

Don't be so darn hard on yourself. You are more beautiful than you think, wiser than you know and created for a greater purpose than you realize. ~Cory Booker (41)

We all die. The goal isn't to live forever, the goal is to create something that will. ~Chuck Palahniuk (42)

Humanology

Humanology is the discovery of the self. ~Natasha Amastar (1)

The sum total of all our human experience is our humanology. ~Don Magyar (2)

One can't live mindfully without being enmeshed in psychological processes that are around us. ~Philip Zimbardo (3)

Without knowing what I am and why I am here, life is impossible. ~Leo Tolstoy (4)

There is a great waste of human possibilities. Each of us must find the causes of that waste. ~Unknown (5)

It isn't what people think that is important, but the reason they think what they think. ~Eugene Ionesco (6)

We don't see things as they are, but we see them as we are. ~Anais Nin (7)

When the mind is at war with itself there are bound to be emotional casualties. ~Blythe Daniel (8)

One evening an old Cherokee told his grandson about a debate that goes on inside people. He said, "My son, the battle between two wolves is inside us all. One is Evil. It is envy, jealousy, greed, arrogance, selfishness, lies, deceit, vanity, superiority and ego. The other is Good. It is joy, peace, love, hope, serenity, humility, kindness, empathy, generosity, truth and compassion." The grandson thought about this for a minute and then asked his grandfather: "Which wolf wins?" The old Cherokee simply replied, "The one you feed." ~Unknown (9)

If you understand human behavior, it can't hurt you as much. ~Carol Plum-Ucci (10)

Emotions are energy in motion. ~Blythe Daniel (11)

Anger is one letter short of danger. ~Unknown (12)

If you are patient in one moment of anger, you will escape a hundred days of sorrow. ~Chinese Proverb (13)

Words are powerful weapons, that's why "words" has "sword" in it. ~Natasha Amastar (14)

Promises mean everything but after they are broken, sorry means nothing. ~Unknown (15)

Never ruin an apology with an excuse. ~Hajar Bessal (16)

Everything you are used to, once done long enough, starts to seem natural, even though it might not be. ~Julien Smith (17)

Do not tolerate abusive people, they are not worth suffering for. ~Kate Neaman (18)

The most common way people give up their power is by thinking they don't have any. ~Alice Walker (19)

Never maintain an unfair relationship, for that devalues your personhood. ~Unknown (20)

It is never your responsibility to please unpleasant people because that is self-induced abuse. ~Unknown (21)

Only little people belittle people. ~Rev Run (22)

Pay no attention to those who talk behind your back. It simply means you are two steps ahead! ~Unknown (23)

How people treat you is their karma; how you react is yours. ~Wayne Dyer (24)

Be mindful of your words so you can be guilt-free, not guilty! ~Jerome Neaman (25)

The people you hurt today will be your teachers tomorrow. ~Natasha Amastar (26)

Hurt people hurt people. ~Unknown (27)

Feelings are never lost they are just misplaced. ~Blythe Daniel(28)

There is no healing without feeling. ~Blythe Daniel (29)

Don't be ashamed to cry, it simply means your heart is working. ~Natasha Amastar (30)

Listen to your pain. It is your greatest teacher. ~Blythe Daniel (31)

When you judge another, you do not define them, you define yourself. ~Wayne Dyer (32)

People are like mirrors; some are empty mirrors who don't see you, others are broken mirrors who see a distorted you, and then there are healthy mirrors who see the true you. ~David Daniel (33)

Don't let someone create you because they might destroy you. ~Unknown (34)

When you keep bad company you face bankruptcy. ~Blythe Daniel (35)

If you find yourself always agreeing with everyone, you haven't found yourself. ~Natasha Amastar (36)

When you say "yes" to others, make sure you are not saying "no" to you. ~Paulo Coelho (37)

If you have to ask yourself if you're happy, you're probably not. ~Unknown (38)

Every man is born an original, but sadly, most men die copies. ~Abraham Lincoln (39)

Auditions are being held for you to be yourself. Apply within. ~Shawn Upchurch (40)

Be yourself; everyone else is already taken. ~Oscar Wilde (41)

YOU are YOUnique. ~Natasha Amastar (42)

We all have a history, but it's not the end of the story. ~Rachel Daniel (43)

Do not meekly let life pass you by, for that is a waste of your having been born. ~Unknown (44)

The human condition needs unconditional love. ~Blythe Daniel(45)

Challenge

From the concrete who knew that a flower would grow. ~Drake (1)

Don't settle for the sky's the limit when there are footprints on the moon. ~Unknown (2)

When you are going through something difficult and are wondering where God is? Remember, the teacher is always silent during a test. ~Unknown (3)

We ask the Great Spirits for strength so they give us difficulties which make us strong. ~Native American Proverb (4)

Unless you try something beyond what you have already mastered you will never grow. ~Ralph Waldo Emerson (5)

We doubt ourselves to protect ourselves. ~Tanner Leiderman (6)

Make failure your teacher, not your undertaker. ~Chris Archer (7)

Problems are not stop signs, they are guidelines. ~Robert Schuller (8)

When someone tells me "No," it doesn't mean I can't do it, it simply means I can't do it with them. ~Karen E. Quinones Miller (9)

Success is the ability to go from one failure to another with no loss of enthusiasm. ~Winston Churchill (10)

The greatest mistake you can make is trying not to make any, because life is a learning process. ~Natasha Amastar (11)

Turn your mess into a message. ~Unknown (12)

We must define ourselves by the best that is in us, not the worst that has been done to us. ~Edward Lewis (13)

We delight in the beauty of the butterfly, but rarely admit the changes it has gone through to achieve that beauty. ~Maya Angelou (14)

The paradox is that when I accept myself just as I am, then I can change. ~Carl Rogers (15)

When you embrace your addiction you can kiss it goodbye. ~Blythe Daniel (16)

Don't practice until you get it right, practice until you can't get it wrong. ~Unknown (17)

Hard work beats talent when talent fails to work hard. ~Unknown (18)

When all is said and done, more is said than done. ~Lou Holtz (19)

Failures are divided into two classes: those who thought and never did, and those who did and never thought. ~John Charles Salak (20)

Nothing will work unless you do. ~Maya Angelou (21)

Find a way, not an excuse. ~Unknown (22)

I've learned that even when I have pains, I don't have to be one. ~Maya Angelou (23)

Whenever I "hurt" I just mix it up and make it "thru." ~Natasha Amastar (24)

There is no greater agony than bearing an untold story inside you. ~Maya Angelou (25)

If I committed suicide I couldn't live with myself. ~Tanner Leiderman (26)

Build bridges around you, not walls. ~Asher Monroe Book (27)

We can each turn on each other or toward each other. ~Unknown (28)

It is in the heart that all wars are won. ~Avatar The Last Airbender (29)

Success is never final and failure is never fatal. It is courage that counts.
~Winston Churchill (30)

Courage is what it takes to stand up and speak; courage is also what it takes to sit down and listen. ~Winston Churchill (31)

In the CHAlleNGE lies the CHANGE. ~Natasha Amastar(32)

The biggest room is the room for improvement. ~Unknown (33)

Turn the cell into a classroom and the prison into a university. ~Khalil Osiris (34)

To me, impossible just means unstoppable. ~Rachel Daniel (35)

If you believe you can, you might. If you know you can, you will. ~Steve Maraboli (36)

The wishbone will never replace the backbone. ~Henry James(37)

Today is a mountain but you were born to climb! ~Unknown (38)

Inspiration

Your life is an occasion. Rise to it! ~Suzanne Weyn(1)

Some men see things as they are and say "Why?" I dream things that never were and say "Why not?" ~Robert F. Kennedy (2)

Nothing is impossible, the word itself says, "I'm Possible." ~Audrey Hepburn (3)

Your "I CAN" is more important than your "IQ." ~Robin Sharma (4)

I am realistic – I expect miracles. ~Wayne Dyer (5)

There are two ways of spreading light: to be the candle or the mirror that reflects it. ~Edith Wharton (6)

Young people need models, not critics. ~John Wooden (7)

If you must raise your voice do it to cheer someone on. ~Unknown (8)

Doubting yourself is a death sentence. Believing in yourself should be your first sentence. ~Natasha Amastar (9)

Regret shapes us but it does not define us. ~Tanner Leiderman (10)

It's never too soon and it's never too late. ~Unknown (11)

Believing in yourself is the highest compliment you can give yourself. ~Blythe Daniel (12)

A pessimist sees the difficulty in every opportunity; an optimist sees the opportunity in every difficulty. ~Winston Churchill (13)

Motivation is when your dreams put on work clothes. ~Benjamin Franklin (14)

I put pressure on myself because pressure makes diamonds. ~Tanner Leiderman (15)

Things turn out best for the people who make the best out of the way things turn out. ~Art Linkletter (16)

Take life as you find it, but don't leave it that way. ~Unknown (17)

Although it takes a million stars, there's enough in you to light up the whole sky. ~Rachel Daniel (18)

YOU are the YOUniverse and everything is within your reach. ~Natasha Amastar (19)

We are all champions in life. Living is the prize! ~Hector David Jr. (20)

There is a crack in everything. That's how the light gets in. ~Leonard Cohen (21)

Never fear shadows, they simply mean there is a light shining nearby. ~Ruth Renkel (22)

Be a rainbow in someone else's cloud. ~Maya Angelou(23)

Turn your wounds into wisdom. ~Oprah Winfrey (24)

Every day I hurt a little less because every day I learn a little more. ~One Life To Live

(25) I don't think of all the misery, but of all the beauty that still remains. ~Anne Frank

(26)   In a world where you can be anything you want... Be Yourself. ~Rev Run (27)

Because you are alive, everything is possible. ~Thich Nhat Hanh (28)

A baby is God's opinion that the world should go on. ~Carl Sandburg (29)

Guidance

Stand with your head held high but always walk with your head bowed. ~Blythe Daniel (1)

Some people are in your life as lessons, others as blessings. Cherish your blessings and learn from your lessons. ~Chris Archer (2)

Let us not look back in anger, or forward in fear, but around in awareness. ~Unknown (3)

Don't go through life, grow through life. ~Eric Butterworth(4)

Do something today that your future self will thank you for tomorrow. ~Barbara Niven (5)

Someday your life will flash before your eyes. Make sure it's worth watching. ~Unknown (6)

Live your life with the end in mind. ~Stephen Covey(7)

Parent your children with their end in mind. ~Blythe Daniel(8)

Watch your thoughts, they become your words. Watch your words, they become your actions. Watch your actions, they become your habits. Watch your habits, they become your character. Watch your character, it becomes your destiny. ~Unknown (9)

Live with integrity and your conscience will thank you. ~Natasha Amastar (10)

Be righteous without being self-righteous. ~Rehab (11)

Every thought, every word, every action you do, bears your signature. ~Thich Nhat Hanh (12)

Your word is the standard you set for yourself. Live up to it. ~Natasha Amastar (13)

The greatest discovery of all time is that a person can change his future by merely changing his attitude. ~Oprah Winfrey (14)

When you're finished changing, you're finished. ~Benjamin Franklin (15)

Live, learn, evolve. ~Chris Archer (16)

Each of us is destined for greatness. To get there sooner do good and be invisible. ~Blythe Daniel (17)

There is nothing better than to be a better person. ~Natasha Amastar (18)

The way to do is to be. ~Lao Tsu (19)

Be both definitions of thoughtful. ~Chris Archer (20)

Observe people with love. ~Blythe Daniel (21)

Do not judge and you will never be mistaken. ~Jean-Jacques Rousseau (22)

Talent is God-given. Be humble. Fame is man-given. Be grateful. Conceit is self-given. Be careful. ~John Wooden (23)

If you think winning is everything, you've already lost. ~Natasha Amarata (24)

Don't be too controlling or life will change when you least expect it. ~Asher Monroe Book (25)

If you have to bring someone down to get to the top, you're still at the bottom. ~Benjamin Kleinman (26)

Never let the hand you hold, hold you down. ~Unknown (27)

Pick friends that fill your mind with matter, not with things that don't matter. ~Blythe Daniel (28)

If you can't change your friends, change your friends. ~Fonzworth Bentley (29)

When you know better, do better, cuz that's how the world gets better. ~Natasha Amastar (30)

It's nice to be important, but it's more important to be nice. ~Unknown (31)

The best accessories are pearls of wisdom and a heart of gold. ~Natasha Amastar (32)

Strive to be deeper than a reflection. ~Kevin Schmidt (33)

BeYOUtiful. ~Unknown (34)

To embrace the journey towards our full potential, we need to become our own loving teacher. ~Osho (35)

Be a knowledge seeker, wisdom keeper, truth speaker, and live deeper. ~Natasha Amastar (36)

Men must live and create. Live to the point of tears. ~Albert Camus (37)

Look at everything as if you were seeing it either for the first or last time. Then your time on earth will be filled with glory. ~Betty Smith (38)

Don't judge each day by the harvest you reap, but by the seeds that you plant. ~Robert L. Stevenson (39)

Live as if you were to die tomorrow, learn as if you were to live forever. ~Mahatma Gandhi (40)

Be a souloist and give the performance of your life. ~Natasha Amastar (41)

There are no ordinary moments. ~Dan Millman (42)

If you want to stand out, be outstanding. ~Romeo Miller (43)

Make your life a standing ovation, then the angels above will give you an encore. ~Natasha Amastar (44)

Life is fragile, handle with prayer. ~Unknown (45)

Service

No one has ever become poor by giving. ~Anne Frank (1)

There's hard work and then there's heart work. ~Usher (2)

A go-getter should also be a go-giver. ~Napoleon Hill (3)

Life's most persistent and urgent question is, "What are you doing for others?"
~Martin Luther King, Jr. (4)

Your greatest possession is not what you have, but what you have to give.
~Natasha Amastar (5)

Each one, teach one. ~Beverly Bond (6)

There is no better exercise for your heart than reaching down and helping to lift someone up. ~Bernard Meltzer (7)

Kindness is the language which the deaf can hear and the blind can see. ~Mark Twain (8)

You may be the bread-winner but the real winner is the one who shares his bread.
~Rachel Daniel (9)

True heroism is not in the urge to surpass others at whatever cost but the urge to serve others at whatever cost. ~Arthur Ashe (10)

Role models think about others before they think about themselves. ~Blythe Daniel (11)

In a world full of people who couldn't care less, be someone who couldn't care more. ~Unknown (12)

Each of us is a guardian angel in training. The more we fulfill our assignments the sooner we will get our wings. ~Blythe Daniel (13)

There is no higher religion than human service. ~Woodrow Wilson (14)

It's not about the "I's," it's about the "U's." ~Natasha Amastar (15)

How wonderful it is that nobody need wait a single moment before starting to improve the world. ~Anne Frank (16)

If I can help someone I'll do it in a heartbeat because that's what makes my heart beat. ~Natasha Amastar (17)

Never look down on anyone unless you are helping them up. ~Chris Archer (18)

Messengers are all around us. Be one of them. ~Blythe Daniel(19)

When you learn - teach, when you get - give. ~Maya Angelou (20)

When we all realize that we are each other's guardian angels there will be heaven on earth. ~Natasha Amastar (21)

We make a living by what we get, but we make a life by what we give. ~Winston Churchill (22)

The best way to find yourself is to lose yourself in the service of others. ~Mahatma Gandhi (23)

The difference you make makes all the difference. ~Natasha Amastar (24)

Service to others is rent you pay for your room here on earth. ~Muhammad Ali (25)

One penny can make a difference, that's why they call it change. ~Unknown(26)

The first question the priest and Levite asked was, "If I stop to help this man, what will happen to me?" But the good Samaritan asked, "If I do not stop to help this man, what will happen to him?" ~Martin Luther King, Jr. (27)

Goodness is the only investment that never fails. ~Henry David Thoreau (28)

It is when we forget ourselves that we do things that will be remembered. ~Unknown (29)

There are these amazing little seeds called compassion. You should grow some. ~Richelle Goodrich (30)

In the end, the number of prayers we say may contribute to our happiness, but the number of prayers we answer may be of even greater importance. ~Dieter Uchtdorf (31)

My passion is compassion. ~Unknown (32)

I'm dedicated to spreading light. It's contagious. ~Alicia Keys(33)

Promise only what you can deliver. Then deliver more than you promise. ~Unknown (34)

We came here to serve not to be served. ~Unknown (35)

The people you need the most in your life are the people that need your help. ~Natasha Amastar (36)

The greatest gift you can give yourself is helping someone else. ~Blythe Daniel (37)

You can give without loving, but you can never love without giving. ~Robert L. Stevenson (38)

To give pleasure to a single heart is better than a thousand heads bowing in prayer. ~Mahatma Gandhi (39)

Compassion is a verb. ~Thich Nhat Hanh (40)

I figured out a long time ago what life is all about. It's not about me. It's about what I can do for you. ~Natasha Amastar (41)

Gratitude

Life is like a mirror. Smile at it and it smiles back at you. ~Peace Pilgrim (1)

Today is a gift, that is why they call it the present. ~Unknown (2)

We are all here to be a blessing and that is why we are blessed. ~Unknown (3)

Receive every gift with humility, for it is the highest form of gratitude.
~Natasha Amastar (4)

If the only prayer you said was "thank you," that would be enough. ~Meister Eckhart (5)

Walk as if you were kissing the earth with your feet. ~Thich Nhat Hanh (6)

With gratitude as my attitude, I thank you. ~Natasha Amastar (7)

Love the life you live. Live the life you love. ~Bob Marley(8)

Now and then it's good to pause in our pursuit of happiness and just be happy. ~Common (9)

We should certainly count our blessings, but we should also make our blessings count.
~Neal A. Maxwell (10)

Some people grumble that roses have thorns; I am grateful that thorns have roses.
~Alphonse Karr (11)

Be thankful for what you have; you'll end up having more. If you concentrate on what
you don't have, you will never, ever have enough. ~Oprah Winfrey (12)

Greatness cannot be achieved with an ungrateful heart. ~Natasha Amastar (13)

Hem your blessings with thankfulness so they don't unravel. ~Unknown (14)

The only people with whom you should try to get even are those who have helped you.
~John E. Southard (15)

Friends are those rare people who ask how we are and then wait to hear the answer.
~Ed Cunningham (16)

People don't care how much you know until they know how much you care. ~Unknown (17)

Feeling gratitude and not expressing it is like wrapping a present and not giving it.
~William Arthur Ward (18)

Three powerful words, "I appreciate you." ~Shawn Upchurch (19)

Saying thank you is more than good manners. It is good spirituality. ~Alfred Painter (20)

How important it is for us to recognize and celebrate our heroes and our she-roes!
~Maya Angelou (21)

When we find someone who is brave, fun, intelligent and loving we have to thank the
universe. ~Maya Angelou (22)

The hardest arithmetic to master is that which enables us to count our blessings.
~Eric Hoffer (23)

When you appreciate kindness, kindness appreciates you. ~Natasha Amastar (24)

A smile is a curve that sets everything straight. ~Phyllis Diller (25)

Wisdom

The only thing that you absolutely have to know is the location of the library.
~Albert Einstein (1)

The major event of life is the day in which we encounter a mind that startles us.
~Ralph Waldo Emerson (2)

A man looks at his life and thinks, "I need more."
A wise man looks at his life and thinks, "I need no more."
But an enlightened man looks at his life and thinks, "I'm needed more." ~Natasha Amastar (3)

He who knows enough is enough will always have enough. ~Lao Tsu(4)

The most important things in life are not things at all. ~Touched By An Angel (5)

Don't gain the world and lose your soul; wisdom is better than silver and gold.
~Bob Marley (6)

Knowledge speaks, but wisdom listens. ~Jimi Hendrix (7)

There is no greater teacher than the lesson. ~Tanner Leiderman (8)

The Universe is my University. ~Natasha Amastar (9)

To be smart is to know. To be wise is to do. ~Blythe Daniel (10)

Life is filled with a billion moments; some you won't want to remember and some you'll never want to forget. Take a moment to learn from them all. ~Matthew King (11)

What lies behind us and what lies before us are tiny matters compared to what lies within us. ~Ralph Waldo Emerson (12)

Every living thing has a soul. How many cells do you have living in your body?
~Blythe Daniel (13)

Life's tragedy is that we get old too soon and wise too late. ~Benjamin Franklin (14)

Life can only be understood backwards, but it must be lived forward. ~Soren Kierkegaard (15)

Humanity makes mistakes, but learning from the mistakes is what makes humanity.
~Natasha Amastar (16)

We must learn together as brothers or perish together as fools. ~Martin Luther King Jr. (17)

Our scientific power has outrun our spiritual power. We have guided missiles and misguided men. ~Martin Luther King, Jr. (18)

I know not weapons World War III will be fought, but World War IV will be fought with sticks and stones. ~Albert Einstein (19)

The choice is not between violence and non-violence, but between non-violence and non-existence. ~Martin Luther King, Jr. (20)

When the power of love overcomes the love of power the world will know peace.
~Jimi Hendrix (21)

There is enough in the world for everyone's need, but not for everyone's greed.
~Frank Buchman (22)

It's more important to enrich your mind than your wallet. ~Jerome Neaman (23)

Abundance is a vibration. It's not a dollar amount in your bank account. ~Jake T. Austin (24)

Some people so poor, all that they've got is money. ~Alicia Keys (25)

If you think you're always right, you're already wrong. ~Giancarlo Stanton (26)

An intelligent person can rationalize anything, a wise person doesn't try to. ~Jen Knox (27)

Learn from the mistakes of others. You can't live long enough to make them all yourself. ~Unknown (28)

The measure of intelligence is the ability to change. ~Albert Einstein (29)

Learning takes learning. ~Martin Leiderman (30)

Make your favorite food, "Food for Thought." ~Natasha Amastar (31)

Define a man by his questions, not his answers. ~Voltaire (32)

Student: "Dr. Einstein, Aren't these the same questions as last year's physics final exam?"
Dr. Einstein: "Yes; But this year the answers are different." ~Albert Einstein (33)

I lost track of time trying to catch up to it. ~Tanner Leiderman (34)

We animals spend most of our lives quarrelling over where we are going in the next life while all the other animals are enjoying this one. ~Sal Palladino (35)

It seems like we can't wait for the future but we want to live in the past. ~Tanner Leiderman (36)

Can't buy back time. Spend yours wisely. ~Jake T. Austin (37)

If I had to live my life again, I'd make the same mistakes, only sooner. ~Tallulah Bankhead (38)

Maturity is simply the wisdom to determine the right time to be a kid and the right time to be an adult. ~Nate Storvik (39)

Age is an issue of mind over matter. If you don't mind, it doesn't matter. ~Mark Twain (40)

Time heals everything, but it also kills everything. ~Tanner Leiderman (41)

I complained because I didn't have shoes until I saw someone without feet. ~Unknown (42)

If you don't humble yourself God will do it for you. ~Natasha Amastar (43)

The saying, "Respect others, you never know who you're talking to" should be, "Respect others, you always know you're taking to a human being." ~Redaric Williams (44)

Worry not that no one knows of you; seek to be worth knowing. ~Confucius (45)

If you have knowledge, let others light their candles in it. ~Margaret Fuller (46)

Light weighs nothing but fills everything. ~Tanner Leiderman (47)

The Universe's energy doesn't lie. ~Kendrick Lamar (48)

Wisdom is truth unaltered. ~Natasha Amastar (49)

All truth is hidden in plain sight. ~David Daniel (50)

A hungry traveler met a wise woman on the road. When she opened her bag to share her food, the hungry traveler saw a precious stone in her bag. Admiring it, the wise woman gave him the stone without hesitation. Rejoicing, he knew the jewel would give him good fortune for the rest of his life. But, a few days later he returned and said to her, "I know how valuable this stone is, but I give it back to you in the hope that you can give me something much more precious. If you can, give me what you have within you that enabled you to give me the stone." ~The Best of Bits and Pieces (51)

The desire to reach for the stars is ambitious. The desire to reach hearts is wise. ~Maya Angelou (52)

What wisdom can you find that is greater than kindness? ~Jean-Jacques Rousseau (53)

There is a reason why the word "evolve" has the word "love" in it. ~Natasha Amastar (54)

Knowledge teaches us to change. Wisdom teaches us to change the world. ~Natasha Amastar (55)

To ignore wisdom is death. ~Blythe Daniel (56)

Consciousness

Consciousness is the key to advancement. Unlock your next level. ~Natasha Amastar (1)

The real history of consciousness starts with one's first lie. ~Joseph Brodsky (2)

The greatest of faults, is to be conscious of none. ~Thomas Carlyle (3)

If we live truly, we shall see truly. ~Ralph Waldo Emerson (4)

Consciousness is the truth, the whole truth, and nothing but the truth.
~Natasha Amastar (5)

Seek first to understand, then to be understood. ~Stephen Covey (6)

To get out of the dark- ask questions. To see clearly- demystify. To not blindly follow-
step out of the line ~Natasha Amastar (7)

In order to doubt existence you have to exist. ~Tanner Leiderman (8)

I think therefore I am. ~Rene Descartes (9)

The unexamined life is not worth living. ~Socrates (10)

Losing an illusion makes you wiser than finding a truth. ~Ludwig Borne (11)

Don't think outside the box... Think like there is no box. ~Unknown (12)

No problem can be solved from the same level of consciousness that created it.
~Albert Einstein (13)

It is a terrible thing to see and have no vision. ~Helen Keller (14)

Life is a nightmare when you're not fully awake. ~Blythe Daniel (15)

It's interesting how we can go from "no where" to "now here" with the slightest shift in consciousness. ~Chris Archer (16)

It is always your next move. ~Napoleon Hill (17)

We all make choices but in the end the choices make us. ~BioShock (18)

The good life is a process. It is a direction, not a destination. ~Carl Rogers (19)

It's not about getting to the light, it's about becoming the light. ~Natasha Amastar (20)

The illusion is we are only physical. ~Vanna Bonta (21)

We are not human beings having a spiritual experience. We are spiritual beings having a human experience. ~Pierre Teilhard de Chardin (22)

Begin to see yourself as a soul with a body rather than a body with a soul. ~Wayne Dyer (23)

Human beings are Soular Powered. ~Natasha Amastar (24)

He who looks outside, dreams; he who looks inside, awakes. ~Carl Jung (25)

Death is a stripping away of all that is not you. The secret to life is to "die before you die" - and find that there is no death. ~Eckhart Tolle (26)

All that matters is what you make matter. Therefore, you make matter. ~Unknown (27)

I am not defined by the DNA in my blood but by the light in my soul. ~Natasha Amastar (28)

Remind yourself to find yourself. ~Redaric Williams (29)

May you live every day of your life. ~Jonathan Swift (30)

At the center of my being is my knowing. ~Natasha Amastar (31)

I cannot tell you any spiritual truth that deep within you don't already know. All I can do is remind you of what you have forgotten. ~Eckhart Tolle (32)

The Truth is inseparable from who you are. Yes, you are the Truth. If you look for it elsewhere, you will be deceived every time. ~Eckhart Tolle(33)

The "Being of Light" is already in you. ~Natasha Amastar (34)

The whole universe exists inside you. Ask all from yourself. ~Rumi (35)

Each day let us wake ourselves. ~Tom Maden (36)

Existence is awareness without boundaries. ~Deepak Chopra (37)

Thanks to impermanence, everything is possible. ~Thich Nhat Hanh (38)

To define is to limit. ~Oscar Wilde(39)

The world is full of magic things, patiently waiting for our senses to grow sharper. ~William Butler Yeats (40)

How can a three-pound mass of jelly that you can hold in your palm imagine angels, contemplate the meaning of infinity, and even question its own place in the cosmos. ~Vilayanur Ramachandran (41)

What does your Soular System revolve around? ~Natasha Amastar (42)

Sometimes I sit and think and other times I just sit. ~Satchel Paige (43)

Conscious breathing is my anchor. ~Thich Nhat Hanh (44)

Meditate for the happiness of others. Even if it doesn't work for them, it will work for you. ~Unknown (45)

Enlightenment is "the light in men." ~Natasha Amastar(46)

Justice

When we embrace each other's differences the world will be one. ~Natasha Amastar (1)

Non-judgment day is near. ~Unknown (2)

Labels are meant for things, not people. ~Natasha Amastar (3)

Justice just is. ~David Daniel (4)

I have no country to fight for; my country is the earth, and I am a citizen of the world. ~Eugene Debs (5)

To me, it seems a dreadful indignity to have a soul controlled by geography. ~George Santayana (6)

We will not be satisfied until justice rolls down like water and righteousness like a mighty stream. ~Martin Luther King, Jr. (7)

Some say this isn't the right time for change, and they are right. It should have been done yesterday. ~Unknown (8)

The obstruction of justice leads to the destruction of the soul. ~Natasha Amastar (9)

Injustice anywhere is a threat to justice everywhere. ~Martin Luther King, Jr. (10)

There is no right way to do the wrong thing. ~Tanner Leiderman (11)

Morality = More Reality. ~Blythe Daniel (12)

When your morality becomes an instinct, you have evolved. ~Natasha Amastar (13)

Justice will not be served until those who are unaffected are as outraged as those who are. ~Benjamin Franklin (14)

If you become conscious of a wrong, make sure your conscience rights it. ~Blythe Daniel (15)

You may be free, but is your conscience? ~Natasha Amastar (16)

The moral arc of the universe bends at the elbow of justice. ~Martin Luther King, Jr. (17)

Right is right, even if everyone is against it and wrong is wrong, even if everyone is for it. ~William Penn (18)

Integrity requires no rules. ~Albert Camus (19)

If you have integrity, nothing else matters. If you don't have integrity, nothing else matters. ~Alan Simpson (20)

The means we use must be as pure as the ends we seek. ~Martin Luther King, Jr. (21)

Few will have the greatness to bend history itself, but each of us can work to change a small portion of events. ~Robert F. Kennedy (22)

We have flown the air like birds and swum the sea like fishes but have yet to learn the simple act of walking the earth like brothers. ~Martin Luther King, Jr. (23)

What a sad era when it is easier to smash an atom than a prejudice. ~Albert Einstein (24)

The Pledge of Allegiance says "liberty and justice for all." Which part of "all" don't you understand? ~Patricia Schroeder (25)

I will not let anyone walk through my mind with their dirty feet. ~Mahatma Gandhi (26)

I must uphold my ideals, for perhaps the time will come when I shall be able to carry them out. ~Anne Frank (27)

There is no higher court than the court of conscience. ~Mahatma Gandhi (28)

I'm for truth no matter who tells it. I'm for justice no matter who it's for. ~Malcolm X (29)

You shall be my witness. ~Yeshua (30)

Human Rights

CIVIL RIGHTS:

We may have all come on different ships, but we're in the same boat now.
~Martin Luther King, Jr. (1)

America did not invent human rights. In a very real sense human rights invented America. ~Jimmy Carter (2)

Man is born free, yet everywhere he is in chains. ~Jean-Jacques Rousseau (3)

The soul that is within me no man can degrade. ~Frederick Douglass (4)

The finest clothing made is a person's own skin. ~Mark Twain (5)

People with clenched fists cannot shake hands. ~Ralph Bunche (6)

The problem with haters is they see my glory, but they don't know my story.
~Maya Angelou (7)

Wherever men and women are persecuted because of their race, religion or political views, that place must, at the moment – become the center of the universe. ~Elie Wiesel (8)

First they came for the Jews and I did not speak out – because I was not a Jew. Then they came for the Communists and I did not speak out – because I was not a communist. Then they came for the trade unions and I did not speak out – because I was not a trade unionist. Then they came for me – and there was no one left to speak out for me.
~Martin Niemoller (9)

There comes a time when silence is betrayal. ~Martin Luther King, Jr. (10)

You can't take back the words you never said. ~Lupe Fiasco (11)

When you stop fighting for what's right, you become what's wrong. ~Natasha Amastar (12)

I do not intend to tiptoe through life only to arrive safely at death. ~Unknown (13)

Don't go with the flow, make waves. ~Natasha Amastar(14)

One has a moral responsibility to disobey unjust laws. ~Martin Luther King, Jr. (15)

Is life so dear, or peace so sweet, as to be purchased at the price of chains and slavery? Forbid it, Almighty God! I know not what course others may take; but as for me, give me liberty or give me death! ~Patrick Henry(16)

I would rather die on my feet than live on my knees. ~Charles Houston (17)

I prayed for twenty years but received no answer until I prayed with my legs.
~Frederick Douglass (18)

The history of the past is one long struggle upward to equality. ~Elizabeth Cady Stanton (19)

With each generation our country must become more equal, not less. ~Tammy Baldwin (20)

Please use your freedom to promote ours. ~Aung San Suu Kyi (21)

First they ignore you, then they laugh at you, then they fight you, then you win.
~Mahatma Gandhi (22)

It is easy to build monuments but harder to build movements. ~Joseph Echols Lowery (23)

Be ashamed to die until you have won some victory for humanity. ~Horace Mann (24)

At the end of the game the king and the pawn go in the same box. ~Unknown (25)

equALLity. ~Unknown (26)

L.I.P. – Live In Peace. ~Cory Booker (27)

For all those whose cares have been our concern, the work goes on, the cause endures, the hope still lives and the dream shall never die. ~Ted Kennedy (28)

WOMEN'S RIGHTS:

It starts when you sink in his arms and ends with your arms in the sink. ~Unknown (1)

Not only is a woman's work never done, the definition keeps changing. ~Bill Copeland (2)

How is it that men are born entitled, but women are given a title? ~Natasha Amastar (3)

Why is he called "Boss" but she's called "Bossy." ~Unknown (4)

I asked a Burmese why women, after centuries of following their men, now walk ahead. He said there were many unexploded land mines since the war. ~Robert Mueller (5)

I do not wish women to have power over men but over themselves. ~Mary Wollstonecraft (6)

I became a feminist as an alternative to becoming a masochist. ~Sally Kempton (7)

Feminism is an entire world view or Gestalt, not just a laundry list of women's issues. ~Charlotte Bunch (8)

We hold these truths to be self-evident: that all men and women are created equal. ~Elizabeth Cady Stanton (9)

Men, their rights, and nothing more; women, their rights, and nothing less. ~Susan B. Anthony (10)

A girl should be two things: who and what she wants to be. ~Coco Chanel (11)

I would have girls regard themselves not as adjectives, but as nouns. ~Elizabeth Cady Stanton (12)

I see my body as an instrument rather than an ornament. ~Alanis Morissette (13)

Teach girls to be supermodels - super role models. ~Natasha Amastar (14)

The test for whether or not you can hold a job should not be the arrangement of your chromosomes. ~Bella Abzug (15)

It is now possible for a flight attendant to get a pilot pregnant. ~Richard Ferris (16)

Women belong in the house... and the Senate. ~Unknown (17)

Men do not own the exclusive right to get angry. Anger is an equal opportunity emotion. ~Blythe Daniel (18)

Men are taught to apologize for their weakness, women for their strengths. ~Lois Wyse (19)

The first problem for us all, men and women, is not to learn, but to unlearn. ~Gloria Steinem (20)

We have to free half of the human race, the women, so that they can help free the other half. ~Emmeline Pankhurst (21)

Every time we liberate a woman we liberate a man. ~Margaret Mead (22)

Be a she-ro. ~Maya Angelou (23)

History is herstory too. ~Unknown (24)

Don't be afraid to pray to God. She is always listening. ~Jake Daniel (25)

AMEN and AWOMEN! ~Unknown (26)

MEN'S RIGHTS:

Men's liberation is a movement that recognizes that men too have been imprisoned by the narrow confines of society. ~Tanner Leiderman (1)

From a young age, boys are taught to be tough and to "be a man," but they aren't men, they are children who need to laugh and cry and just be. ~Alicia Robbins (2)

People say, "real men don't cry." The truth is, "real men" do cry and those who don't are hurting. ~Jake Daniel (3)

Feel sad for the man who can't cry, for there is a little boy inside of him still waiting to. ~Natasha Amastar (4)

If you tell a boy to "suck it up," he will, and that's the problem. He swallows his feelings and chokes on them for the rest of his life. ~Corra King(5)

Tape the sound of your baby son crying. Let him listen to the tape when he is going through pain as a grown man. ~Yoko Ono (6)

When a boy is told not to play with dolls he is being told that a baby is not his responsibility. ~Blythe Daniel (7)

A boy's body must be protected at all times. Boys are just as vulnerable as girls. ~Lewis Scott (8)

When a boy is molested by a woman, he did not "get lucky," he did not "score," and it is not "cool." RAPE IS RAPE! ~J.T. Junior (9)

By the time a boy becomes a man society has robbed him of his humanity. ~Alan Madden (10)

Being a man can be hazardous to his health. He is driven to succeed (road rage), he must climb his way to the top (hypertension), and, if he fails (drowns himself in alcohol). All this, because society conditions him to be the alpha male. ~David Daniel (11)

Men hurt too and their hurt needs to be heard. ~Alan Madden (12)

Men who feel keep it real. ~Natasha Amastar (13)

The men's liberation movement frees a man from having to be the badboy, the playboy, and the homeboy. Instead, he can be a genuine person who doesn't have to prove anything. ~Blythe Daniel (14)

What a relief that I don't have to play sports, drink beer, or act tough and, I am still a man. ~Jake Daniel (15)

Manhood should not be defined by the stereotypes of society; the machismo, the gigolo and the CEO, but by one's M.O.; Merit Only. ~Natasha Amastar (16)

When men learn to flex their heart muscle as much as their other muscles, they will discover their true strength. ~Blythe Daniel (17)

We need more films that send positive messages to boys: that cooperation is heroic and respecting women is as manly as defeating the villain. ~Hector David Jr. (18)

Fellas, step your brain up, not your game up. ~Redaric Williams (19)

Once a man is liberated he can be a real role model; kind, caring, affectionate and not ashamed of telling his children, "I love you." ~Jerome Neaman (20)

Give your son hugs and kisses so he will be able to give them back to the kids and the Mrs. ~Mickey Rashad (21)

There are many good fathers who are denied custody of their children when they are the most-fit parent. ~David Daniel (22)

Men's liberation starts in the home when a boy is allowed to cry and comes full circle when he cries tears of joy while holding his newborn baby. ~Matthew King (23)

CHILDREN'S RIGHTS:

There can be no keener revelation of a society's soul than the way in which it treats its children. ~Nelson Mandela (1)

No social problem is as universal as the oppression of the child... No slave was ever so much the property of his master as the child is of his parent... Never were the rights of man ever so disregarded as in the case of the child. ~Maria Montessori (2)

No one is more truly helpless, more completely a victim, than he who can neither choose nor change nor escape his protectors. ~John Holt (3)

Hitler, Stalin, Mao and other dictators were exposed to severe physical mistreatment in childhood and refused to face up to that fact later. Instead of seeing and feeling what had happened to them, they avenged themselves vicariously by killing millions of people. And millions of others helped them to do so. ~Alice Miller (4)

There was never a time when a major social problem was solved by beating a child. And there never will be such a time... for centuries adults have injured children and have lied about it, and other adults have heard those lies and then merely turned away. ~Surgeon General Dr. C. Everett Koop (5)

With three million new cases of child abuse reported each year, we must ask ourselves, "When will this holocaust end?" ~Natasha Amastar (6)

If we treated our friends the way we treat our children, we wouldn't have any friends. ~Unknown (7)

Some parents love their anger more than they love their children. ~Unknown (8)

Bullying is a learned behavior, so don't teach it to your kids. ~Matthew King (9)

If you want to stop violence in the community, you must first stop it in the home. ~Blythe Daniel (10)

It takes a whole community to save a child. ~Dave Pelzer (11)

It is easier to build strong children than repair broken men. ~Frederick Douglass (12)

A child, like all other human beings, has inalienable rights. ~Lucretia Mott (13)

Children will be the last of God's creations to be granted personhood. ~David Daniel (14)

Children are newer and smaller, but not lesser. ~Blythe Daniel(15)

We worry about what a child will become tomorrow, yet we forget that he is someone today. ~Stacia Tauscher (16)

Every child has the right to be raised right; with love, laughter, and the pursuit of happiness. Anything less is unconstitutional. ~Freya Neaman(17)

Biology is the least of what makes someone a mother. ~Oprah Winfrey (18)

Be a better parent than your parent was to you. ~Alicia Robbins (19)

Your children need your presence more than presents. ~Jesse Jackson (20)

Children should be seen, not hurt. ~Unknown (21)

A child's body is their temple. No Trespassing Allowed! ~Natasha Amastar (22)

A child's feelings, no man should degrade. ~Blythe Daniel(23)

Telling children what they should and shouldn't feel takes away their selfhood. ~Natasha Amastar (24)

Validate your child's feelings so your child will grow up feeling of value. ~Rachel Daniel (25)

Leave beauty marks, not scars. ~Blythe Daniel (26)

A parent is the most important mirror a child will ever look into. ~Natasha Amastar (27)

I didn't grow up in my mother's shadow, I grew up in her light. ~Guy Johnson (28)

Teach children to speak up, not shut up. ~Blythe Daniel(29)

We teachers can only help the work going on, as servants wait upon a master. ~Maria Montessori (30)

There are two lasting bequests we can hope to give our children. One of these is roots, the other, wings. ~Hodding Carter (31)

Childhood is a journey, not a race. ~Unknown (32)

Teaching kids to count is good, but teaching kids what counts is better. ~Unknown (33)

Live so that when your children think of fairness, caring and integrity, they think of you. ~Unknown (34)

Whatever it is you want from children, you must give them. ~Unknown (35)

Children are natural Zen masters; their world is brand new in each and every moment. ~John Bradshaw (36)

Every child you encounter is a divine appointment. ~Wess Stafford (37)

Children are the living messages we send to a time we will not see. ~John Whitehead (38)

Do not despair, every newborn baby is a potential prophet. ~R. D. Laing (39)

Look up to the people that came before us... but more importantly, look after the people who will lead us. ~Natasha Amastar (40)

If we are to reach real peace in this world, we shall have to begin with the children. ~Mahatma Gandhi (41)

First they chained us, then they whipped us, then they spanked us. Now, it's time to love us. ~Kids Are Next (42)

Graffiti Walls

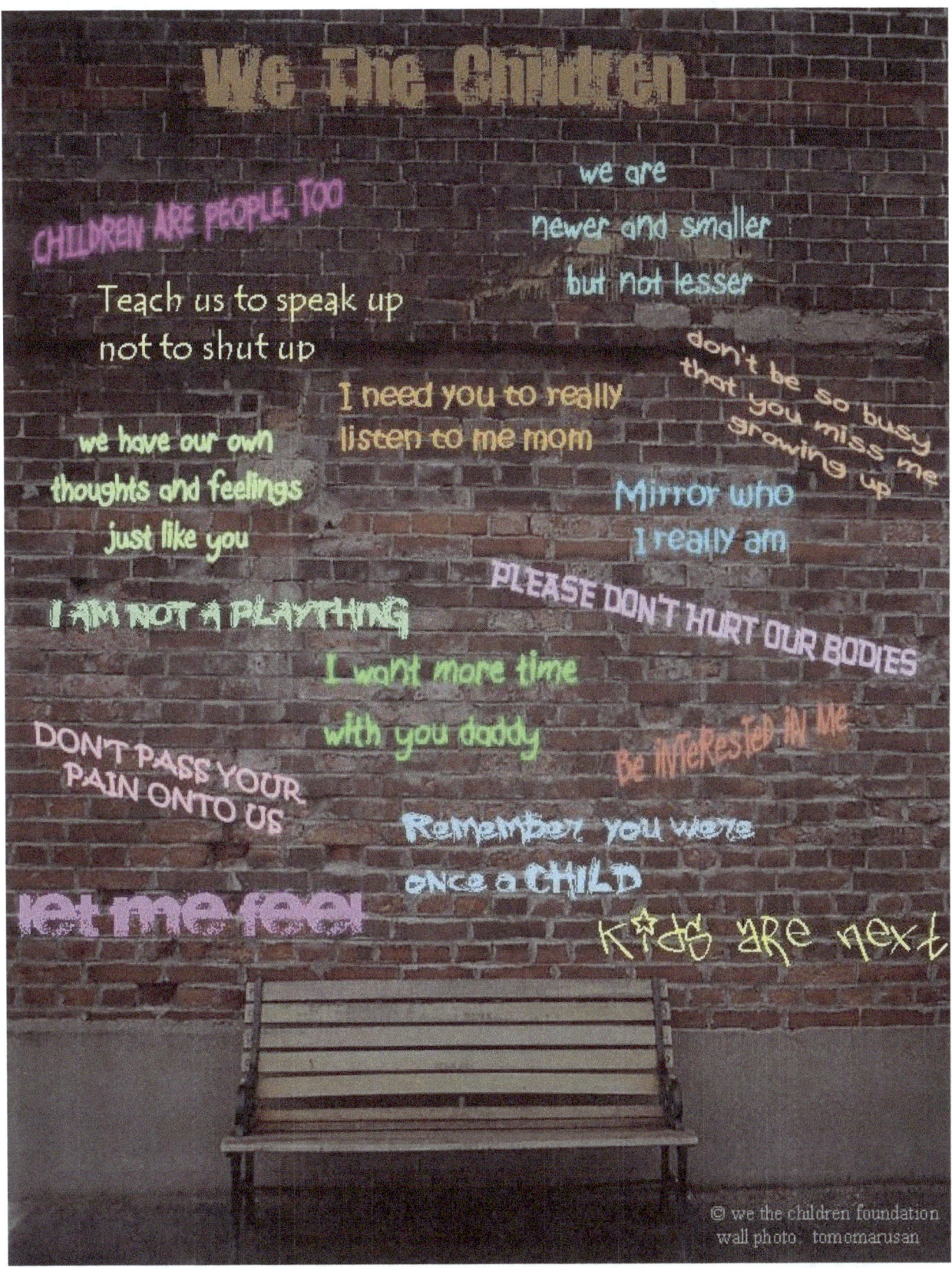

We The Students

I am fragile so handle me with care

Be patient with me
I am learning as fast as I can

When I raise my hand
I'm really trying to
raise my self-esteem

Don't have "FAVORITES"
cuz then I can't be special too

Saying "THIS IS MY CLASSROOM"
makes me feel small

Help me find
my own truth

TALK WITH ME – NOT AT ME

Children NEED more MODELS
than CRITICS

Praise me often
and I will learn to love myself

The classroom isn't
for your emotional agenda

Saying "You won't AMOUNT to anything"
means you have FAILED as a teacher

PLEASE TAKE ME SERIOUSLY

IF YOU MUST RAISE YOUR VOICE
DO IT TO CHEER US ON

teacher, write this on
the blackboard ten times:
I will respect each and every one of you

Some Students Fail Classes
But Some Teachers Fail Students

Be The Stepping Stones
That Lead Me Up The Mountain

I need you more
than you WILL EVER KNOW

I will be one of your
greatest accomplishments

We The Teachers

The ABC's of teaching:
LOVE CHILDREN

we want your time here
to be the happiest days of your life

You can do it!

I am here for you

I will never
give up on you

Some days will be better than others
I'm here for the others

COME to me
my door is always OPEN

WE MAKE A
GREAT TEAM

Each day I look forward to
spending more time with you

YOU CAN COUNT ON ME TO:
1. LISTEN TO YOU +
2. GUIDE YOU +
3. USE MY HEART WHEN YOURS IS BROKEN

I'm So LuCKy I GeT TO be YoUR TEACHER

If I ever hurt you
tell me
so I can apologize

I want to BUILD you UP
not BREAK you DOWN

I want to be your fondest memory
not your worst nightmare

I love watching
you GROW

if you need help
don't be afraid to ask

When I look in your eyes
I know why I am here

I am learning just like you

© we the children foundation
wall photo: emilie eagan

42

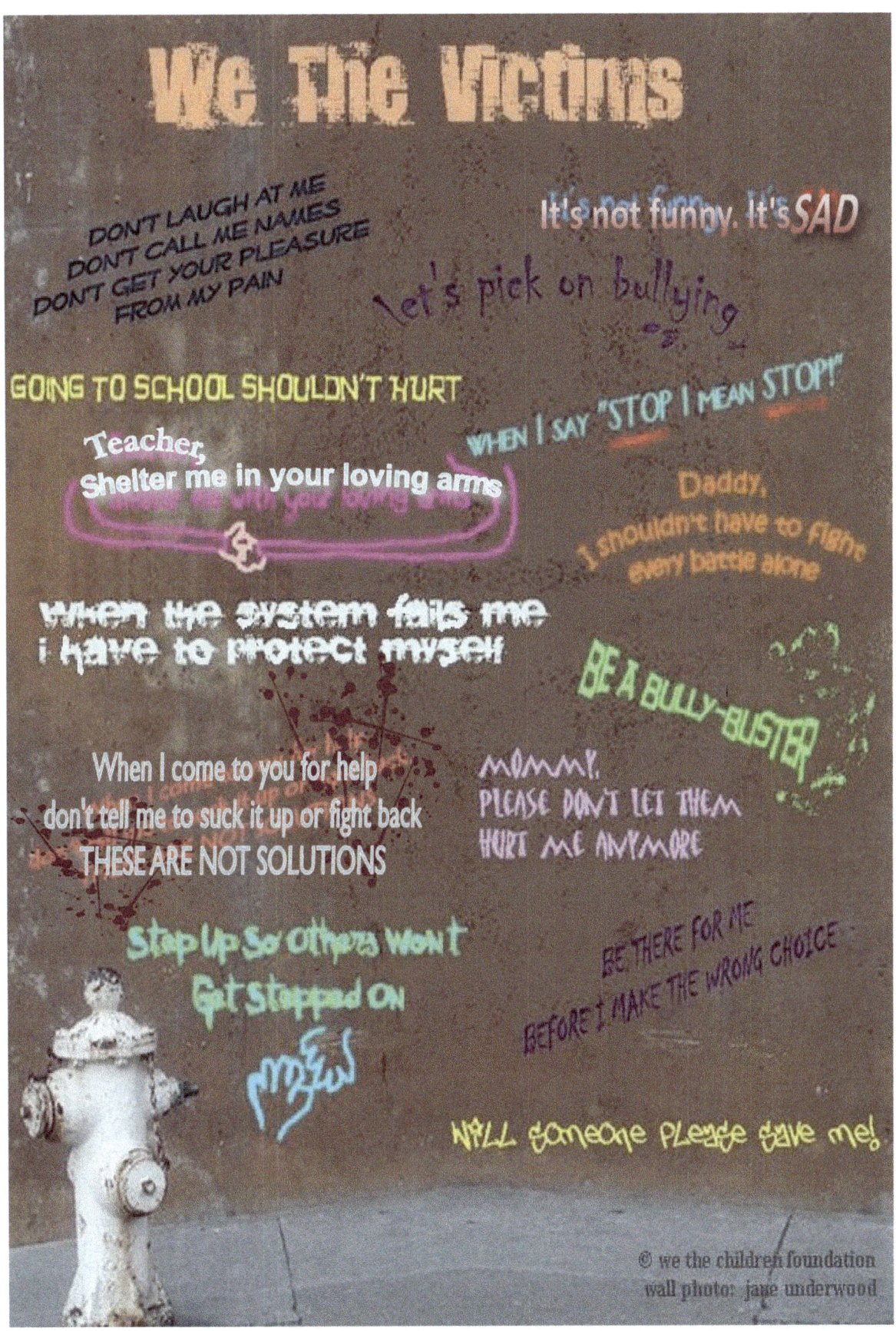

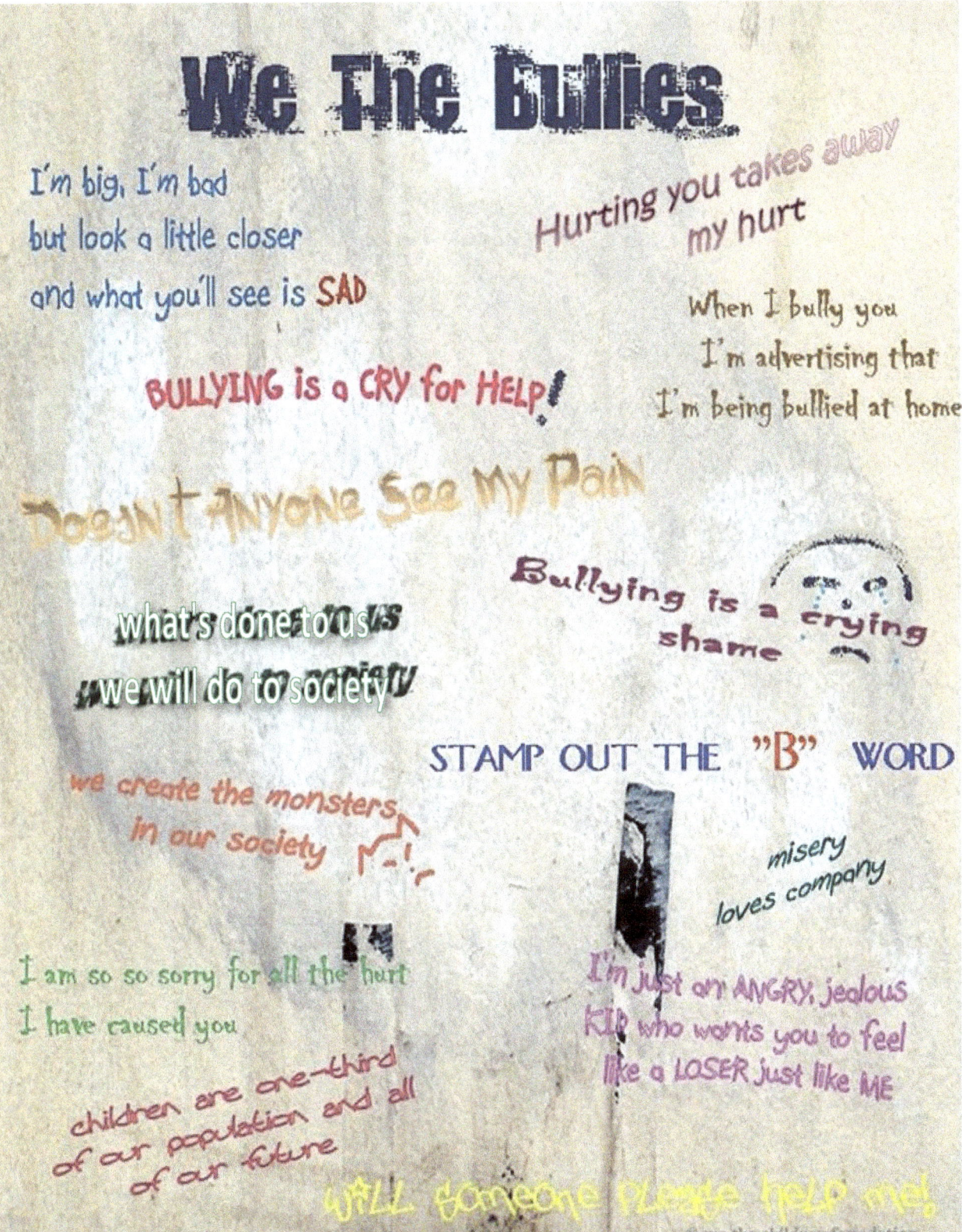

We The Bullies

I'm big, I'm bad
but look a little closer
and what you'll see is SAD

Hurting you takes away
my hurt

When I bully you
I'm advertising that
I'm being bullied at home

BULLYING is a CRY for HELP!

Doesn't ANYONE See My Pain

what's done to us
we will do to society

Bullying is a crying
shame

STAMP OUT THE "B" WORD

we create the monsters
in our society

misery
loves company

I am so so sorry for all the hurt
I have caused you

I'm just an ANGRY, jealous
KID who wants you to feel
like a LOSER just like ME

children are one-third
of our population and all
of our future

WILL someone please help me!

© we the children foundation
wall photo: jane underwood

44

Q uestion
U nderstand
O bserve
T ouch
E nlighten
S erve

When you share your goodness withothers
your life is a quote! ~Natasha Amastar